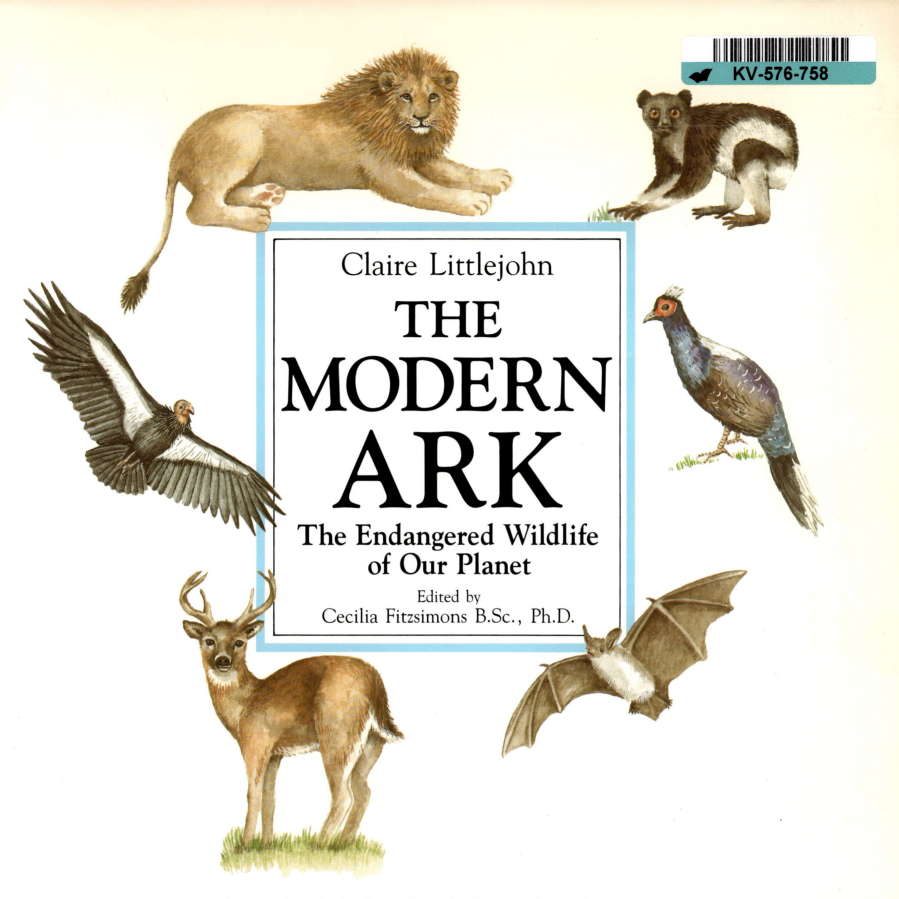

Claire Littlejohn

THE MODERN ARK

The Endangered Wildlife of Our Planet

Edited by
Cecilia Fitzsimons B.Sc., Ph.D.

The animals in this book are all at risk. Those "endangered", or at serious risk, are marked (E) in the text. Those that are vulnerable to becoming endangered are marked (V). Some animals are increasingly rare, but not yet endangered. They are marked (R). Those animals about which little is known and which may be endangered are marked (K).

WORLD INTERNATIONAL PUBLISHING LIMITED
MANCHESTER

Tropical Forests

Ocelot

Woolly
Spider Monkey

Imperial Amazon Parrot
Amazona imperialis

Location: Dominica

There are 271 species, or kinds, of parrots. Many are threatened by man. Parrots are popular cage birds and, as many people like to collect rare ones, the parrots' chance of survival is not good. The biggest threat to them is the uncontrolled cutting down of the world's tropical and subtropical forests. Parrots, such as the imperial Amazon, that live on islands are the most endangered. They are few in number, slow to breed, and less adaptable to changing habitats. (E)

Sumatran Tiger
Panthera tigris sumatrae

Location: Sumatra

The tiger preys on large animals living in fairly thick forests. Tigers usually hunt alone. Each male tiger's hunting area, however, includes the separate territories of several females. The major threat to the tiger's survival is the increasing lack of its large prey and dense cover, both greatly reduced by man's need for more farmland. The tiger, which was widespread from the Caspian Sea, through India, south east Asia and eastern China, is now only found in isolated pockets. The Sumatran tiger is one of eight subspecies. It is smaller than the Indian tiger, with stripes that are closer together. (E)

Northern Pudu

Rufous-headed Ground Roller

Queen Alexandra's Birdwing Butterfly

Hercules Beetle

Philippine (Monkey-eating) Eagle

Aye-Aye
Daubentonia madagascariensis
Location: Madagascar

The aye-aye is the only species in its family: one of the eleven families of primates. It lives only in the northern part of Madagascar's east coast rain forest. A very strange-looking animal, it has long guard hairs on its body, hairless, bat-like ears and very big front teeth that are separated from the few others. It has a thin middle finger on each hand which it uses to extract insects from holes or crevices. Active only at night, it sleeps in a nest by day. The aye-aye's teeth are always growing. They are constantly being worn down by the animal's habit of chewing through the shells of coconuts and other fruits, and ripping off the bark of trees to get at larvae. The aye-aye is threatened by the destruction of the rain forest but it is also killed because some local people regard its strange appearance as an evil omen. (E)

Orang-Utan
Pongo pygmaeus
Location: N. Sumatra & Borneo

A large ape with long red hair, the orang-utan lives and travels mostly in the trees. The animal uses its long arms, heavy body, and hands and feet which are shaped like hooks, to swing from branch to branch. It has strong teeth and jaws which it uses to open shells and nuts and to chew coarse vegetation. The orang-utan eats a huge amount – mostly fruit – but also leaves, shoots, bark and insects. Solitary in habit, it is also very intelligent. Although the orang-utan is now protected by law, it is still threatened by the disappearance of the rain forest, because of logging and clearing the land for farming. (E)

Cape Mountain Zebra

Short-tailed Chinchilla

Mountains

Swinhoe's Pheasant

Mountain Gorilla
Gorilla gorilla beringei

Location: E. Zaire, W. Rwanda, S.W. Uganda, 5,450-12,500 ft (1660-3810m)

The gorilla is the largest living primate. It lives mainly on the ground and walks on the soles of its feet while balancing on the knuckles of its hands. Only a few hundred of the family of mountain gorillas survive. The other two races, one in West Africa, the other in the east, are both vulnerable. The cutting down of the forest timber, crop-growing and grazing for farm animals has reduced the gorillas' habitat. Poachers hunt the animals for skulls and skins, and trap them for zoos which also threaten their survival in the wild. (E)

Mountain Lion (Cougar)
Felis concolor

Location: U.S.A. & Canada

One of three main species of large wild cats found in North America, the mountain lion, also called cougar, puma or catamount, is the largest. Both the Eastern cougar and Florida cougar are endangered. Cougars adapt to many different habitats and range widely in search of prey. Male and female mountain lions hunt separately. They are found from Canada to South America in wild forests, grassland and desert. The main threat to their survival is hunting by man. They are occasionally shot or trapped as pests. Destruction of their habitat also reduces their chances of survival. (E)

Pyrenean Ibex

Indris

Snow Leopard

California Condor

Spanish Imperial Eagle
Aquila adalberti

Location: Spain & Portugal

The Spanish imperial eagle is the most endangered European bird. Reduced areas of suitable habitat, hunting by man, and poisoning by agricultural chemicals threatens many birds of prey with extinction. Many European countries and North America have laws to protect all birds of prey from hunting and several toxic pesticides have been replaced with less poisonous ones. But it is difficult to preserve the large areas of hunting territory, needed by many birds of prey, in areas of dense human population. Habitat destruction is still the most serious threat to these birds. (E)

Giant Panda
Ailuropoda melanoleuca

Location: W. China, Szechuan Province, 8,500-12,500 ft (2590-3810m)

Very rare but well known, the giant panda was adopted as the symbol of the World Wide Fund for Nature. Although related to racoons, it is bear-like with striking black-and-white markings. Its territories in central and western China are isolated and inhospitable, but are still being reduced by man. Human settlement around its territories also prevents giant pandas moving to new areas for food. Its main food is bamboo and when some species flowered recently and then died back, many animals were unable to find new sources of bamboo. Starvation is the main risk to the giant panda. (R)

Rivers

Japanese Crane

Bog Turtle

Common Sturgeon

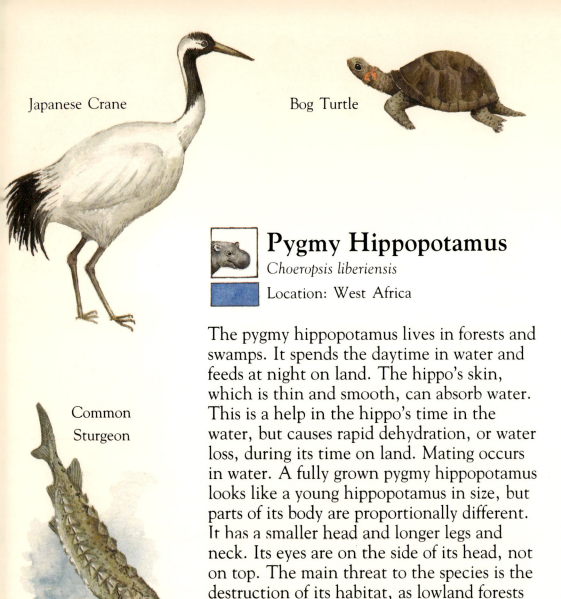

Pygmy Hippopotamus
Choeropsis liberiensis

Location: West Africa

The pygmy hippopotamus lives in forests and swamps. It spends the daytime in water and feeds at night on land. The hippo's skin, which is thin and smooth, can absorb water. This is a help in the hippo's time in the water, but causes rapid dehydration, or water loss, during its time on land. Mating occurs in water. A fully grown pygmy hippopotamus looks like a young hippopotamus in size, but parts of its body are proportionally different. It has a smaller head and longer legs and neck. Its eyes are on the side of its head, not on top. The main threat to the species is the destruction of its habitat, as lowland forests and swamps are cleared and drained for agriculture. (V)

American Crocodile
Crocodylus acutus

Location: U.S.A., Caribbean, Central America

Crocodiles are the largest of the three orders of crocodilians, which also include alligators and gharials or gavials, and caimans. There are 14 species of crocodiles, and all of them are threatened. The main threat to their survival is posed by man. American crocodiles breed late in life and many are killed by hunters before they reach maturity, mate, and raise young. Trade in crocodile skins has been reduced by laws now but it has already led to a great reduction in crocodile numbers. Land reclamation, swamp draining, flooding and other predators on eggs and young also reduce numbers. The American crocodile lives in estuaries and is tolerant of salt water. (E)

Indus River Dolphin

Shining Macromia
Dragonfly

Goliath Frog

Bald Eagle

Pyrenean Desman
Galemys pyrenaicus

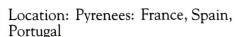
Location: Pyrenees: France, Spain, Portugal

The desman is a close relative of the mole, but has a very different way of life. It is aquatic. The desman's body has adapted for swimming, with long legs and feet, webbed toes and partly webbed fingers and waterproof fur. Its nose and ears can also be closed against the water. The desman relies a great deal on touch, with sense whiskers on its muzzle, tail and legs. Desmans are restricted to the Pyrenees and Russia. All groups are threatened: the Pyrenean desman by trapping and the destruction of its habitat, caused by the damming of mountain streams. Their food supply is found in water: shrimps, snails, insects and larvae and water pollution is an added major threat to their survival. (V)

Giant Otter
Pteronura brasiliensis

Location: South America

The giant otter has suffered a sharp fall in numbers. This is a result of the trade in its skins. Although now protected, poaching continues to pose a serious threat to the giant otter's survival. So does the development of the South American rain forest, with resulting destruction of its habitat and increased pollution of the rivers in which it lives. The giant otter is now the rarest of all otters, but is still found in most South American countries. It is also the largest otter, with a strong seal-like head. Fully grown, it is about 5 1/2 to 6 feet (1.8m) long. Giant otters prefer shallow waters, chasing and catching their prey under water. They are a social species who live in large families and often hunt in pairs or groups. (V)

W. African Manatee

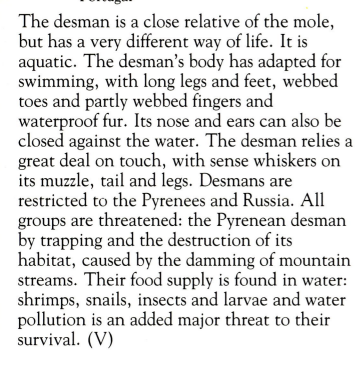

Spanish Lynx

West Virginia
White Butterfly

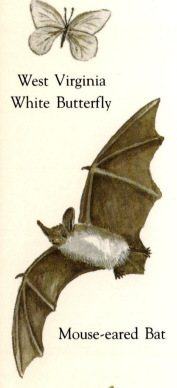
Mouse-eared Bat

Woodlands

 ## Red-cockaded Woodpecker
Picoides borealis
Location: U.S.A.

This species of woodpecker is threatened by the loss of its very specialised habitat. It lives in pine forests or pine and oak woodlands in the south eastern part of the U.S.A. It makes a nest hole only in a large living pine that has rotting wood. It then drills small holes around the nest opening, which allow pine pitch to drip out. This both repels predators and also identifies the nest tree. Woodpeckers have strong claws, short legs and a wedge-shaped stiff tail. These help them climb trees and balance for pecking, which they use to make nest holes, find insects and spiders for food and signal their territory. Woodpeckers help to keep insect numbers under control and aid the decay of dying wood. (V)

 ## Delmarva Fox Squirrel
Sciurus niger cinereus
Location: U.S.A.

The fox squirrel belongs to the same family as the prairie dog. Squirrels are one of the most common animals, with several different body shapes and needs that allow them to live in a wide range of habitats. Despite this variety, some of the nearly 300 species are at risk. The fox squirrel is hunted as a game animal in the United States and this is the major threat to its survival. All squirrels are at some risk from being shot. They are often thought of as pests, because they strip bark from trees, eat young tree shoots and disturb the soil. (E)

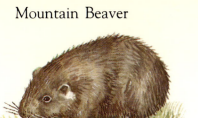
Mountain Beaver

Cerambyx
Longicorn Beetle

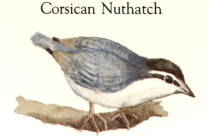
Corsican Nuthatch

Key Deer

Great Peacock Moth
Saturnia pyri

Location: Austria, West Germany, Czechoslovakia

The world has 150,000 to 200,000 species of moths and butterflies. There are very small ones, with wingspans of 1/10 inch (0.3cm), and giants with wingspans of 12 inches (30cm). The great peacock moth is Europe's largest. Its wingspan is up to 6inches (15cm), but this is still dwarfed by the Atlas emperor moth of Asia with a 12inch (30cm) wingspan. All the emperors have bold eyespots on the wings and lack the proboscis or sucking "tongue" that is the most common feature of adult moths. Both the male and female great peacock fly at night (not all moths do) and they are often mistaken for bats. They feed on a variety of trees and rest on them in the day. The wing markings help to camouflage them. Habitat loss, the use of toxic pesticides in agriculture and acid rain all threaten their survival. (E)

Grey Wolf
Canis lupis

Location: N. United States, Canada, Europe, Asia

Attacks on people by wolves are rare. But stories of attacks are common. It is both fear of the wolf and the destruction a pack can cause to farm stock that lead to persecution by people. Habitat destruction is the other major cause of the wolf's decline. The grey wolf was once the most common mammal, apart from man, in the non-tropics. It is now found only in some Eastern European forests, isolated mountains of the Mediterranean, mountains and near deserts of the Middle East and wilderness areas of North America and Asia. The grey wolf is the largest member of the dog family. It is very adaptable, with different sizes and colour in changing habitats. (V)

Periodical Cicada

Asiatic Lion

San Diego Horned Lizard

Deserts

Red-kneed Tarantula

Arabian Oryx

Oryx leucoryx

Location: Oman

Once common in Arabia, Jordan, Iran and Iraq, the oryx was hunted to extinction in the wild by the early 1970s. After the Second World War, hunters used automatic weapons and vehicles in place of ancient rifles and camels, with deadly results. Herds survived in captivity and were reintroduced to Oman in the 1980s. The oryx is well suited to the hostile conditions of the desert. A nearly all-white coat reflects the sun's heat. Flat, wide hooves allow it to walk, rather than run, on sandy surfaces for long periods. It is not aggressive and does not, as a result, waste energy, while it shares available shade with others. Herds also have a clear social dominance order. This helps overcome the difficulty of mate finding, predators and suitable habitat. (E)

Ridge-nosed Rattlesnake

Crotalus willardi

Location: Mexico & U.S.A.

There are just under 2,500 species of snakes in eleven families. Snakes are found throughout the world, except the Arctic, Antarctica, some small islands and Iceland, Ireland and New Zealand. Members of the viper family, which includes just under 10 per cent of the snake population, use speed and venom on their prey. Pit vipers, a group that includes rattlesnakes, have a deep pit between the nostril and the eye on either side of the face. These have sensitive nerve ends that detect infra-red heat rays. The snake can both detect an animal and judge its distance. Each time a rattlesnake sheds its skin, it adds a horny part to the tail. This it vibrates when disturbed to give the "rattle". The snakes are killed from fear and for the use of their skins in fashion items. Habitat change is another threat to their survival. (E)

Pakistan Sand Cat

African Wild Ass

Grevy's Zebra

Wild Bactrian Camel
Camelus bactrianus
Location: Mongolia, China

Egyptian Tortoise
Testudo kleinmanni
Location: Egypt, Israel, Libya

Camels have been used widely by nomadic peoples as beasts of burden and for their milk, meat and wool. Three of the six species of camel, including the one-humped dromedary camel of Arabia and Africa, are domesticated. The Bactrian, or two-humped, camel was domesticated as long ago as 2,500B.C. Changes in human settlement, with enforced ending of nomadic societies in its territories, has reduced numbers drastically to the small surviving wild populations in Mongolia and the trans-Alti Gobi Desert. They are of slender build, with short brown coats in summer that are longer and shaggier in winter. They eat a wide variety of plants but can survive long periods without food as they have fat reserves in their humps. They also can go long periods without water. (V)

Tortoises are one of the 13 families of turtles and tortoises. There are 41 species of tortoise, half of which are endangered. Tortoises are found in tropical and subtropical regions on all the major land masses except Australia and Antarctica. In many of these regions they have been caught and killed for food. The developed nations have added to the risk to their survival by importing tortoises as pets. The Egyptian tortoise has a non-rigid shell. They have evolved a hinge on the lower part of the shell covering the belly. This allows the shell to be completely closed to give added protection and prevent loss of body moisture. (V)

Giant Kangaroo Rat

Desert Rat-Kangaroo

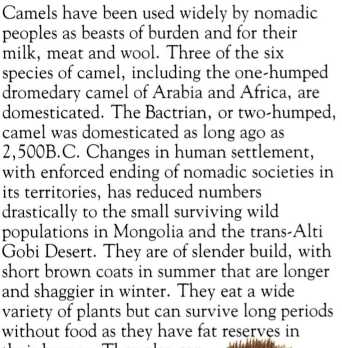

Grasslands

Przewalski's Horse

Swayne's Hartebeest

Noisy Scrub-Bird

Great Bustard
Otis tarda

Location: N. Europe & N. Asia

Bustards can fly but they live mainly on the ground on the open plains of Africa, Australia and Eurasia. The great bustard is scattered from Europe, through Russia and into China. These birds are easily frightened and desert their nests if disturbed. With grasslands giving way to farming, human disturbance is a major cause of their decline. Pesticides and fertilizers have also been very damaging. The great bustard has a spectacular courtship display. It inflates its neck, brings its tail forward onto the back and stretches its wings to reveal white secondary feathers. Then, its normal camouflage is replaced by easily seen, nearly all-white feathers. (R)

Great Indian Rhinoceros

Rhinoceros unicornis

Location: India & Nepal

The Indian rhino looks as if it is wearing armour. Its skin is grey, hairless and bumpy, with many folds. Like all rhinos it feeds on plants, grazing over several square miles on the grasslands of the Indian floodplains. Indian rhinos also spend a lot of their time in water. They are quite aggressive and will often rush at intruders. Man has been a threat to the rhino since the last century, and the main reason for the continuing decline of the animal is poaching. There is a large demand for rhino horns, for their supposed magical properties. (E)

Brown Hyena

Pronghorn

European Bison

Cheetah
Acinonyx jubatus

Location: Africa, Middle East, Iran, & U.S.S.R.

Poaching and habitat loss are the two main threats to the cheetah's survival. Although protected, the demand for skins to make coats is high. And the reduced size of the cheetah's hunting territory, with fewer available prey, leads to starvation and attacks on farm livestock. Farmers then kill cheetahs as pests. The cheetah is, in brief spells, the fastest land animal. It has a slim body with a flexible spine and this gives it great acceleration. The cheetah uses this burst of speed (up to 60mph or 100kph) at the end of a stalk for prey that can last minutes or hours. (V)

Utah Prairie Dog
Cynomys parvidens

Location: U.S.A.

The prairie dog is one of nearly 300 species of squirrel. Squirrels are widespread and have adapted physically in behaviour to suit many different habitats. Prairie dogs breed once a year. Unusually both male and female prairie dogs are friendly towards their young in the first summer of life and share in their care. Half the prairie dog's life is spent growing to full adult size. They live underground in social groups, several groups living side by side over a large area. In summer the boundaries between them are relaxed, but in winter they are defended by each one's dominant male. They feed near the burrow, clearing tall plants to give a wide view and cropping plants and grass short. As well as natural predators, man can be an enemy, especially where habitat is reclaimed for agriculture. (V)

African Wild Dog

Large Blue Butterfly

Oceans

Harbour Porpoise

Queen Conch

Audouin's Gull

Dugong

Yellow-eyed Penguin
Megadyptes antipodes

Location: New Zealand

The 16 species of penguin live in the
southern hemisphere. Three are at risk. The
largest numbers are found around the coast
of Antarctica, and the widest range of species
in New Zealand. Among them is the yellow-
eyed. This has declined in numbers because
of human development in the coastal dunes
where it breeds and the reduction of dense
vegetation. All penguins are at risk from oil
pollution and commercial fishing. They
have few natural enemies on land, even
though they cannot fly. They are superb
swimmers and divers. Waterproof feathers
and a layer of fat keep them warm in near
freezing waters. (E)

Loggerhead Turtle
Caretta caretta

Location: All temperate and
subtropical seas

Two of the 13 families of turtle, live in
the oceans – the six species of sea turtles that
have streamlined, armour-plated shells, and
the leatherback sea turtle that has a shell
without plates. Sea turtles cannot retract
their heads into their shells. The loggerhead
is the biggest and heaviest of the family,
growing up to 7 feet (2 metres) long. The
loggerhead is a flesh eater, feeding on
mussels, crabs, barnacles, sea urchins and
fish. Five of the six species of sea turtles are
at risk. Exploitation, pollution and habitat
destruction are the main threats. Turtles
have been killed for food and for their shells.
Because they lay their eggs on beaches at
certain regular times, the females and their
eggs are at risk from all enemies, including
human ones. Many nesting beaches have
been developed for tourism. (V)

Japanese Sea Lion

Red Coral

Humpback Whale

Short-tailed Albatross

European Lobster

Homarus gammarus

Location: N.E. Atlantic & N. Europe coastlines

There are nearly 40,000 species of crustaceans. Their bodies are covered with a hard shell or crust and usually divided into segments. The shell moults for growth. The limbs are jointed. They live mainly in water. Common crustaceans are lobsters, crabs, shrimps and barnacles. Fossil records reveal crustaceans lived on earth over 500 million years ago. Lobsters walk along the sea bottom on their four rear pairs of legs. The first, front pair are powerful claws for attack and defence. They are flesh eating scavengers, living in holes on rocky bottoms. They can grow to 2 feet (60cm) in length and survive up to 100 years. Pollution and commercial over-fishing are the main threats to this and the American lobster, *Homanus americanus*. (E)

Mediterranean Monk Seal

Monachus monachus

Location: Mediterranean and Mauritanian coasts.

There are three families of seal. The monk seal belongs to the true seal family. True seals are slow movers on land, flexing their bodies to lever them forward, but in water they are superb swimmers and divers. They use sideway swings of the hindquarters and their long, broad-webbed feet to swim. The monk seal's main population is in the Aegean and east Mediterranean. Monk seals are most at risk from human interference. If disturbed, pregnant females will leave the isolated beaches where they give birth for less safe spots and nursing mothers will leave their pups. Tourism and development have driven the seals from beaches to hidden caves and reduced both breeding and resting habitat. Intensive fishing has reduced its food supply and fishermen kill the seals because they feed on the limited fish stocks. Ten countries border its territory and co-operation between them is essential. (E)

Polar Regions

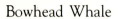
Bowhead Whale

Southern Right Whale

Glacier Bay Wolf Spider

 ## Narwhal

Monodon monoceros

Location: Northern polar waters

The narwhal is one of two species of white whale. It is a striking sight. The skin colour is dramatic – a mixture of grey-green, cream and black splashes. But the unicorn horn is spectacular. The narwhal has only two teeth and the left one continues to grow and forms the counter-clockwise spiral tusk. It grows up to three metres long, and is over half the body length of the whale. It pushes out from the left upper lip and points left and down at the same time. Hunting is one major threat to the narwhal. The tusk is prized by hunters for sale to collectors. Increased mining and oil exploration in the Arctic and new hydroelectric schemes all have a serious effect on the narwhal's habitat. (K)

 ## Laptev Walrus

Odobenus rosmarus laptevi

Location: Laptev Sea, Russia

The walrus is one of the three families of seals. Walruses live only in the Arctic ocean and surrounding ice-covered seas. The walrus has two unusual physical features: ivory tusks and a thick skin. Both male and female walruses develop tusks. The animal with the largest tusks is usually the dominant walrus. The thick skin gives protection from injury from the tusks of other walruses. As walruses often lie on top of each other when resting out of the water, this is useful! The walrus swims by paddling with the rear limbs. It goes slowly along the bottom in shallow water and digs out food with its nose. Walruses are an essential part of the Eskimo economy. Past and present hunting for the ivory tusks, skins and oil have reduced numbers.
(K)

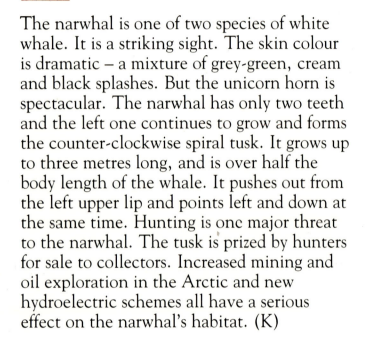